CW00368995

Mind, Body & Soul

ZEN THOUGHTS & QUOTES
TO INSPIRE INNER PEACE

Do not dwell in the past.
Do not dream of the future.
Concentrate the mind on the
present moment.

BUDDHA
Indian spiritual leader
(approx. 563 BCE – 483 BCE)

LAKE PRESS

Lake Press Pty Ltd
16 Sandilands Street
South Melbourne VIC 3205 Australia
Email: publishing@lakepress.com.au
www.lakepress.com.au

Copyright © Lake Press Pty Ltd, 2012
Images used under license from Shutterstock.com and Thinkstock.com
All rights reserved

Design: Canary Graphic Design

First published 2012
Printed in China 5 4 3 2
LP14 128

Preface

Do some emotional housekeeping! We have to take care of our mind, body and soul for it to flourish, for us to live life well. To promote good health and physical and mental wellbeing, we try meditation, yoga, the latest health supplements, massage, detox programs and even psychic readings.

Now you can use this book and music to lighten your heart and ease your mind. *Mind, Body & Soul* can provide solace and inspiration to those in need of support or just give pleasure to those who enjoy the peace it evokes.

We know what your mind and body is, but what is a soul? In certain spiritual, philosophical or psychological traditions, it is the incorporeal essence of a person, living thing or object. Many philosophical or spiritual systems teach that humans have souls, and others teach that all living things and even inanimate objects, like rivers, have souls. Soul sometimes functions as a synonym for spirit, mind or self.

Zen is all about wisdom and the attainment of enlightenment. Spiritual enlightenment is the gradual process of soul evolution that leads to increasing degrees of understanding and awareness of your own reality. In other words, it is a key to the peace of mind that we all crave.

Let these quotes and thoughts inspire and educate you to rejuvenate your body, enrich your mind and nourish your soul. In short, use them to live life well through the holistic integration of health, lifestyle and inner beauty.

Nothing can cure the soul but the senses,
just as nothing can cure the senses but the soul.

OSCAR WILDE
Irish writer and poet (1854–1900)

You don't have a soul.
You are a soul.
You have a body.

C.S. LEWIS
British writer (1898–1963)

The soul is not where it lives,
but where it loves.

UNKNOWN

Teach us delight in simple things.

RUDYARD KIPLING
English poet (1865–1936)

Nothing is worth more than this day.

JOHANN VON GOETHE
German writer (1749–1832)

Zen is the exploration of reality.
It is about your life in the place where you live,
here and now.
It is this immediacy that gives it its strength.

ROBERT ALLEN
Canadian-American author (1948–)

The miracle is not to fly in the air,
or to walk on the water:
but to walk on the earth.

CHINESE PROVERB

*If you understand, things are just as they are;
if you do not understand, things are just as they are.*

ZEN PROVERB

*Faith is the daring of the soul
to go further than it can see.*

WILLIAM NEWTON CLARKE
American author (1841–1912)

Do not dwell in the past.
Do not dream of the future.
Concentrate the mind on the present moment.

BUDDHA
Indian spiritual leader (approx. 563 BCE – 483 BCE)

Love not what you are,
but what you may become.

MIGUEL DE CERVANTES
Spanish author and poet (1547–1616)

Within yourself is a stillness and a sanctuary
to which you can retreat at any time
and be yourself.

HERMANN HESSE
German-Swiss poet and author (1877–1962)

I drink tea and forget the world's noises.

CHINESE SAYING

Silence is a friend who will never betray.

CONFUCIUS
Chinese philosopher (551 BCE –479 BCE)

Sit quietly, doing nothing,
spring comes,
and the grass grows by itself.

ZEN WISDOM

*The mind's first step to self-awareness
must be through the body.*

GEORGE SHEEHAN
American author (1918–1993)

The quieter you become the more you are able to hear.

ZEN SAYING

Walking is Zen, sitting is Zen.
Whether talking or remaining silent,
Whether moving or standing quiet,
The Essence itself is ever at ease.

DAISHI
Japanese monk (774–835)

Sit

Rest

Work.

Alone with yourself, never weary.

On the edge of the forest live joyfully,

without desire.

BUDDHA
Indian spiritual leader (approx. 563 BCE – 483 BCE)

*We must always change,
renew, rejuvenate ourselves;
otherwise we harden.*

JOHANN VON GOETHE
German writer (1749–1832)

Your vision will become clear only when you can look into your heart.
Who looks outside, dreams.
Who looks inside, awakens.

CARL JUNG
Swiss psychiatrist (1875–1961)

Arranging a bowl of flowers in the morning can give a sense of quiet to a crowded day – like writing a poem or saying a prayer. What matters is that one be for a time inwardly attentive.

ANNE MORROW LINDBERGH
American aviator and author (1906–2001)

Each soul must meet the morning sun,
the new sweet earth, and the Great Silence alone!

CHARLES ALEXANDER EASTMAN
Native American author (1858–1939)

When I begin to sit with the dawn in solitude,
I begin to really live.
It makes me treasure every single moment of life.

GLORIA VANDERBILT
American author (1924–)

Take care of your body.
It's the only place you have to live.

JIM ROHN
American author (1930–2009)

There is a silence into which the world
cannot intrude.
There is an ancient peace you carry
in your heart and have not lost.

A COURSE IN MIRACLES
American self-study curriculum

Be not afraid of growing slowly.
Be afraid of standing still.

CHINESE PROVERB

The foolish reject what they see,
not what they think.
The wise reject what they think,
not what they see.

ZEN SAYING

*If our nature is permitted to guide our life,
we grow healthy, fruitful and happy.*

ABRAHAM MASLOW
American psychologist (1908–1970)

Come forth into the light of things,
let nature be your teacher.

WILLIAM WORDSWORTH
English poet (1770–1850)

Beneath, the mountain stream flows on
and on without end.
If one's Zen mind is like this,
seeing into one's own nature cannot be far off.

HAKUIN
Japanese Zen Buddhist (1686–1768)

To see a World in a grain of Sand
And a Heaven in a Wild Flower,
Hold Infinity in the palm of your hand
And Eternity in an hour.

WILLIAM BLAKE
English poet (1757–1827)

Every small positive change we make in ourselves
repays us in confidence in the future.

ALICE WALKER
American author and poet (1944–)

The only way to make sense out of change
is to plunge into it,
move with it and join the dance.

ALAN WATTS
British philosopher (1915–1973)

The most valuable thing we can do for the psyche,
occasionally, is to let it rest, wander,
live in the changing light of a room,
not try to be or do anything whatever.

MAY SARTON
American author (1912–1995)

Our bodies are apt to be our autobiographies.

FRANK GELETT BURGESS
American author (1866–1951)

The goal of a healthy solitude is love;
love and acceptance of ourselves as we are
and where we are,
and love and compassion for others.

DOROTHY PAYNE
American philanthropist (1887–1968)

*The real voyage of discovery consists
not in seeking new landscapes
but in having new eyes.*

MARCEL PROUST
French author (1871–1922)

The body is your temple.
Keep it pure and clean for the soul to reside in.

B.K.S. IYENGAR
Indian Yoga founder (1918–)

To keep the body in good health is a duty,
otherwise we shall not be able
to keep our mind strong and clear.

BUDDHA
Indian spiritual leader (approx. 563 BCE – 483 BCE)

There are only two ways to live your life.
One is as though nothing is a miracle.
The other is as though everything is a miracle.

ALBERT EINSTEIN
German physicist (1879–1955)

*Write it your heart that every day
is the best day of the year.*

RALPH WALDO EMERSON
American essayist and poet (1803–1882)

Three things are essential:
great doubt, great faith and great perseverance.

ZEN SAYING

Zen in its essence is the art of seeing into the nature of one's being, and it points the way from bondage to freedom.

D.T. SUZUKI
Japanese author (1870–1966)

Each morning sees some task begun,
each evening sees it close.
Something attempted, something done,
has earned a night's repose.

HENRY WADSWORTH LONGFELLOW
American poet (1807–1882)

Ask not what tomorrow may bring,
but count as blessing every day that Fate allows you.

HORACE
Roman poet (65 BCE – 8 BCE)

You do not need to leave your room.
Remain sitting at your table and listen.
Do not even listen, simply wait.
Do not even wait, be still and solitary.
The world will freely offer itself to you to be
unmasked, it has no choice.
It will roll in ecstasy at your feet.

FRANZ KAFKA
German author (1883–1924)

Life is change. Growth is optional. Choose wisely.

KAREN KAISER CLARK
American inspirational speaker

Washing dishes is not only a Zen exercise,
but you get the dishes clean too.

ROBERT ALLEN
Canadian-American author and speaker (1948–)

The purpose of life, is to live it,
to taste experience to the utmost,
to reach out eagerly and without fear for newer
and richer experience.

ELEANOR ROOSEVELT
American First Lady (1884–1962)

To get rid of your passions is not nirvana –
to look upon them as no matter of yours,
that is nirvana.

ZEN SAYING

Only in growth, reform and change,
paradoxically enough, is true security to be found.

ANNE MORROW LINDBERGH
American aviator and author (1906–2001)

Past and future are illusions.
They exist only in the present,
which is what there is and all that there is.

ALLAN WATTS
British philosopher (1915–1973)

*The true value of a human being
can be found in the degree
to which he has attained liberation from the self.*

ALBERT EINSTEIN
German physicist (1879–1955)

He who knows he has enough is rich.

LAO TZE
Mystic Chinese philosopher

The one and all.
Mingle and move without discriminating.
Live in this awareness and you'll stop worrying
about not being perfect.

SENG TSAN
Chinese patriarch

You must have been warned against letting the golden hours slip by;
but some of them are golden only because we let them slip by.

JAMES M. BARRIE
Scottish author (1860–1937)

An inch of time is an inch of gold: treasure it.
Appreciate its fleeting nature—
misplaced gold is easily found,
misspent time is lost forever.

LOY CHING-YUEN
Chinese Taoist tai chi master (1873–1960)

Do not seek the truth.
Only cease to cherish the opinions.

ZEN SAYING